THE BOOK OF FRANK Debbie Marsh

Enjoy Debbie Marsh

The Book of Frank

Lessons Learned by the Kindergarten Teacher

By Debbie Marsh

Dedication

I dedicate this book to my three children, Sarah, Tori and Matthew. They drive me crazy, insult me, torture me, ignore me, embarrass me and remind me each and every single day about what unconditional love *really* means. I know they love me - painfully, against their will and whether they like it or not. They say it, show it, hide it, regret it and then ultimately, I know they'll rejoice in it. (I just hope I live long enough to see it.)

This labor of love, my darlings, was for you.

THE BOOK OF FRANK Debbie Marsh

Acknowledgments

I want to say *first and foremost* that this is a work of fiction. It is comprised of many incidents that may or may not have happened during my last 26 years of teaching. It is a fictional year in the life of a teacher. Sure, it could be any and each of my last 15 years but that's the reason I adore my job and wouldn't change it for anything in the world. (Except perhaps at the end of each month when it's time to pay the bills.)

I want to thank Frank, Stanley, George, Charlie, Ruthie, Suzie, Sash, Lily and all the darlings whom I've been so very, very lucky to teach over the years. I've learned almost as much from them as I hope they've learned from me. Their joy and love of life made me want to go to work each and every day, and helped me laugh even when I wanted to cry. They each have a very special place in my heart and whether they're teachers, doctors, lawyers, beauticians, scientists, mechanics, waiters or waitresses – I'm so very proud of each and every one of them – and wish them all only the best and the most joyous of lives.

I want to thank the author Sara Henry for tirelessly editing my numerous drafts and pushing me to hit the publish button. Her unwavering support has meant so very much to me. (It's not as if she was busy writing a book or two herself.) I also want to thank Sheila, Patti, Betse, Cassandra, Karen, Cindy, Carly, Sharon, Elaine and all my incredible friends here in town who've put up with my endless "I'm ready to publish" promises these last two years and never rolled their eyes; at least not in **front** of me.

I want to also thank Lisa, Courtney, Cheryl, Lynn, Carol, Linda, Lori, Cindy, Carly, Nicole and Rene for providing me with even more funny stories on Friday afternoons at the local watering hole during our "curriculum" meetings. (Okay, Rene, you weren't actually present for those meetings, but your stories kicked ass.)

And finally, thanks to Sarah, Suzy, Jill, Sherri, Elyse, Sarah, Sheila, ChiTown, Nap, Anne, Kate C-H, Maggie, Maggie2, Ann, Denene, Jane, Eric, Cora, Brian, Rene, Kevin, Leslie, Sharon, Amy, Braja, Sandi, Gigi, Neil, Amy, Clark, my bloggy husband Kevin and MaryAnne. I'm sure I've forgotten several hundred other writers/bloggers who have lifted me up over the years and I'm sorry if I neglected to name you. You've laughed with me in the good times, and held my hand when I was crying. (And because I'm a blubbering idiot, that was plenty of hand-holding.) There are no words.

And, because I can't pay attention for very long, here goes; the long promised *Book of Frank*.

Enjoy.

Introduction

They never told me about him during those many exhausting months I spent earning my teaching degree in southern California. They never told me about the boy whose voice would reach across the school and grab my heart like a vice, who would send me home crying many times during the first six months of school, and who would find a way into my heart like no one else ever had. This particular creature phenomenon was kept a secret, hidden away in a closet only to be freed at the perfect moment.

I spent four years attending a university in Pennsylvania, graduating with a degree in journalism. I invested another six months taking classes about teaching music, gym and health before being accepted into a prestigious teaching program at San Diego State University. While participating in this challenging program, I learned the fundamentals of managing classroom behavior, behaviorist learning theories, cognitive theories of learning, and constructivism in the classroom. I vaguely remember the words pedagogy, Piaget, and transformative intellectual.

During the past twenty-six

years of actual teaching, these are the important things I've learned how to do:

- Tell who had Mexican food for dinner after one quick walk through around the room.
- Quiet a room in three claps and three snaps.
- Tie ten pairs of shoes in less than two minutes—double knotted.
- Recall the first name of any previous student one minute into a conversation.
- Read aloud a picture book, reach into my pocket and hand a child a tissue for a large deposit while never missing a beat. That took some practice.
- Fly across the room with a garbage can in less than fifteen seconds to catch the vomit without knocking over any kids.
- Tell who's an only child after two hours in a room with twenty-five five-year-olds.
- Get permanent marker, glitter glue, paint, and colored pencil mark off any table in the classroom. I know where the janitor hides the good stuff.

- Know who's decided to "borrow" the Lego-man for the night after one quick glance around the group that is sitting criss cross applesauce on the carpet.

- Swoop down, make the pick-up, and swing the child around who's ready to cry after her mommy left. Sometimes we even make it to the prize box. Whoever said bribery doesn't work has never worked with children.

- Steer a conversation from animals to mammals to rabbits having babies to baby sisters to something not appropriate and back to animals smoother than any NASCAR driver out there. (Let's see Dale Earnhardt Jr. do that!)

But four years of undergrad studies, twelve months of teacher training, and twenty years as a teacher in many classrooms—nothing prepared me for the boy named Frank.

Nothing.

THE BOOK OF FRANK Debbie Marsh

Lesson one

He came into my room under extreme duress.

"Ms. Marsh, your new student is here." I barely recognized the voice over the ceiling loudspeaker in our classroom. It was our secretary, Mrs. Sets-Them-Straight. Her voice was accompanied by the crying and wailing of what sounded suspiciously like banshees in the background. Now I've never actually heard the scream of a wild banshee, but I was convinced this is what it would sound like.

This did not sound promising.

I left my room in the capable hands of Mrs. Jones, the paraprofessional who had learned to dodge vomit, clean undistinguishable gooey substances from tables, and stare a child into confessing to a classroom crime within two minutes. She is worth her weight in gold— which isn't very MUCH, but she packs a punch.

As I made my way down the hall towards the office, the wails of the banshee grew louder and louder. I passed various people in the hallway who looked just as confused as I was, since we try very hard to not torture children in our elementary school.

I stood in front of the glass door to the office, and my eyes immediately landed on the source of the screeches.

Huddled under the front of the elaborate secretarial station was what appeared to be a wild boy recently rescued from the forest. Only this one had a Mohawk, a brand-new set of school clothes, and a voice that could wake the dead.

His name was Frank.

Lesson learned: Wear protective gear on the first day of school, or earplugs.

Lesson two

Each morning in kindergarten we participate in something called "The Morning Meeting." It's an activity from *The Morning Meeting* book- a publication from The Responsive Classroom Approach. It's designed to start the day with a bang.

We begin with a greeting, and the children learn how to shake their partner's hand, look them in the eye and say, "Good morning," and use the child's name. It's important that each child hear his or her name, and that each person in the room is greeted.

We play a quick game, go over the schedule of the day, and then participate in "telling sharing."

While this particular part of morning meeting was designed so that we could get to know each other, it has become the most *exciting* part of the day…at least for the teacher and any other adults who might find their way into our classroom.

After our greeting the sharing began.

"My mommy and daddy got in a big fight last night because my dad hit my mom's car in the driveway. She called him lazy and dad got angry and threw the bag of potato chips."

"Oh… one time I ate potato chips!"

"My dad got poker chips for his birthday."

"It was my mom's birthday last week."

"My mom's too."

"Hey, my birthday is in the next season."

"Today is the second day of the season of fall."

"I fell off my bed last night."

Frank added, "Yeah, well LAST NIGHT I saw a deer in the yawd, and I walked up to it and PUNCHED IT IN THE FACE. It went UNCONSHUS."

Me, reeling only slightly: "Okay. Well, class, I think that's enough sharing for today. I'm a little dizzy."

Lesson learned: The morning meeting, it's kind of like a tilt-a-whirl.

Lesson three

He was short and wide and looked a bit like a barrel with a Mohawk. He spoke with a gravelly voice that reminded me of a grandfather who had spent too many years smoking cigarettes. On his arms he proudly sported several press-on tattoos, which were partly worn off in such a way that you couldn't tell if they were tattoos or remnants of the previous evenings' escapades around the neighborhood. He wore a skull and cross-bones necklace that I'm convinced came from a bubble-gum machine and conveniently matched the various skull t-shirts he wore to school every day.

He left the carpet in the middle of lessons whenever he pleased, never raised his hand, spent an inordinate amount of time in the bathroom, told the most outrageous tall tales every morning during telling sharing, and never, ever missed a day of school. I decided that even the germs are afraid of him. He never remembered his library book and brought in bones from road kill for show and tell.

He would talk incessantly during library and even cut his hair with the scissors in art class. He got caught by the gym teacher peeing outside during gym class and would sneak

19

out and hide in the bathroom during music. The only person he would respond to, the only one he would hug each day and pretend to listen to was his classroom teacher.

Apparently, I was the chosen one.

But when I said he "listened" to the teacher, I only meant that he heard me. Because it seemed like he never, really, ever listened.

Lesson learned: It might look and sound like you're talking, but some people will never hear a word you say.

Lesson four

A quick note from the teacher to all customers who were unfortunately shopping at the College Avenue Giant Supermarket Monday afternoon during the first kindergarten field trip of the year:

Thank you for not minding the noise and chaos as the children, led by our resident ringleader, RAN to the free samples in the bakery department. We hope you didn't try any of the samples that were left in the doughnut hole container, and we're sorry that Frank sneezed into it.

We apologize if we knocked anyone over as we played a raucous game of follow the leader with our fabulous tour guide Jon, who informed us his ONLY rule was no touching. I knew he'd regret that.

I want to apologize to the elderly gentleman who dropped his milk when he saw Frank's face on the shelf inside the cooler. Thanks for being such a good sport, and I'm glad that wasn't an actual heart attack you were having.

To the workers behind the seafood counter, I am sorry that the children began chanting "Save the lobster" when you were filling an order for a shocked customer. I know you believe me now when I tell you that there is NO stopping a chant once it gets started.

To the young lady who thought she was cleaning up a water spill in the fresh fruit and vegetable section, we'll just let you believe that. We are currently potty training a child who we THOUGHT was potty trained and have discovered each of the last sixteen days that he is not. Obviously SOMEONE forgot to make him go to the bathroom before we left. And when I say someone, I mean me.

To the girl who had to rebuild the tall pyramid of two-liter Canada Dry Ginger Ale bottles, sorry. Boys CANNOT keep their hands off each other and love to play WWF when the teacher isn't looking. Sorry about the one bottle that exploded.

To the gentleman who jokingly commented to me as I was leaving, "Teachers don't get paid nearly enough."

You are right.

Lesson learned: Invite Frank's mom on all the rest of our field trips; i.e. beg her to come.

22

Lesson five

Every year at the end of August, I can feel the vibrations around the neighborhood. You know, the time of year when parents of school-aged children are doing the happy dance. Oh, I know the happy dance—I'm doing the happy dance myself! I might be the teacher, but I am also a mom. I have three children of my own, who are attending the high school and the middle school. The happy dance comes at the end of a long, fun-filled summer: a summer filled with wet bathing suits, mildewed beach towels, empty wallets, fresh cut grass tracked across your hardwood floors, endless sleepovers, pool dates, golf dates, play dates, and movie dates.

Parents are ready for school to start and, frankly, so are most of the teachers. Come on teachers, you know we are. We have a pretty good idea what *you* are thinking at the end of the summer, but here's a glimpse into what we are thinking.

Come the middle of August, my batteries are re-charged, and I am thinking ahead to the coming year. What kind of group will I get? Will anyone cry on the first day? Will I cry on the first day? Will they hit each other? Can they write their names, stand in a line, fasten their pants, raise their hands, speak English, listen when I'm talking, and more importantly, find the bathroom in time? Will I have the child in my class who forces me to re-think the sabbatical option?

As I brush these questions aside, I begin to think about what a teacher's goals are for the year. Our most important goal is to help children love school. We want them to wake up in the morning excited about the coming day, and at the end of the day we want them to want to come back! And it would be nice if we looked forward to coming back, too. We want them to learn to be kind to their classmates, their teachers, and their friends. We want them to not be afraid to try something new and to not be discouraged if they fail. To that end, I manage to make at least two or three mistakes a day just to be a good role model for them. We want them to be curious about their world, be inquisitive, and be open to new ideas. We want them to take turns, to share, to play fair and we want them to want to learn.

On a more personal note, there are certain goals I have for myself. This year, I would like to make it to school in the actual car I purchased for myself, and not the beat-up '89 Honda Accord that was intended for my seventeen-year-old daughter. Okay, it was free. I would like to make it to school without spilling my coffee all over the floor of said Honda, or my clothing. Psst...always wear something brown or black. It would be nice to make it through the day without getting called to the principal's office for an honest yet catastrophic mistake. I will try to not take my students early to art or music, or pick them up late. The special teachers tend to frown upon that. In addition, I want to be sure to clean up all the glitter, play dough, paint splatters, and permanent marker before the janitor shows up. It would be nice to have him in my corner this year.

Lesson learned: Prepare for unexpected storms that might be named Hurricane Frank. They may come your way and blow your goals right out of the water.

Lesson six

Today during Morning Meeting we spent a good deal of time sharing what we had done over the long five-day weekend.

I watched knowingly as Frank was intent on trying to figure out how to position the rubber band he had discovered on the rug around his dirty, stubby fingers. I could tell by the way he held his hand and my bazillion years of teaching experience that he was about to shoot someone.

Little did I know it would end up being himself.

RIGHT in the squinty eye he was using to guide his shot.

Even at five the kids learn, all on their own, that karma can sometimes sneak up on you and shoot you in the eye.

Lesson learned: Sometimes you have to sit back and let someone else teach the lesson.

Lesson seven

Each morning in our kindergarten classroom the kids participate in literacy centers designed to help them become readers. The children are split into four groups and spend twelve minutes (thanks to a trusty timer) at each of the four literacy centers. Two of the centers are led by yours truly and Mrs. Jones, (cue the music), and the other two are what I try to call "independent centers" (aka two free-for-all centers).

Today in centers while I was working with one of my reading groups, I couldn't resist asking John (aka *Jae-hyun*) about what language he spoke at home. Of course, I KNOW he speaks Korean, but I always take an opportunity to encourage him.

"John, your mommy and daddy told me that you don't like to practice your English at home. You even have your sister Susie who speaks PERFECT English to help, but you won't practice with her. Is that right?"

"I don't know to speak English," he replied.

"John, we are speaking English right now."

"No, I don't know English!" he said, as he shook his head.

"This IS English. You ARE speaking English!" I insisted.

"I don't know English. What   is English?"

"THIS is English. We. Are. Speaking. English."

"No. I don't know dat."

And at that point I couldn't decide if I was Abbott or Costello.

Lesson learned: Some days I think that perhaps I'm the one speaking Korean.

Lesson eight

While being incredibly distracted by Frank, I've hardly had time to remember that I have three children of my OWN who have been feeling a bit neglected. Last night, however, they conspired to remind me of why I love then so.

First, my almost teenaged son Matthew shattered the ceiling light in the stairwell that leads from the kitchen to the basement. It seems he really IS taller than the stairwell, and when he tripped towards the bottom his hand went up to catch himself, and shattered the huge bulb into a million pieces. I wasn't home at the time, but after he realized he wasn't hurt, he actually cleaned the mess up HIMSELF! With a SHOP-VAC! I still can't believe it. I'm still wondering about the empty band-aid box and the wrappers strewn across the kitchen, though.

Second, middle daughter Tori began the week a scary, screaming, emotional wreck. I won't go into the sordid details, but whatever you do, do NOT mention the letters PMS or PCOS or look her in the eye. She's finally back to normal, and thanks to the mind-erasing machine she has built into her brain she doesn't seem

30

to remember treating us all like crap all week. I predict about three weeks of peace until it starts again.

Third, eldest (but not wisest) daughter Sarah reminded me that we had to go to the District Magistrate tomorrow to beg forgiveness for her lapse in judgment while at a late-night party last month. With any luck, she'll get her driver's license back just in time to leave home on her eighteenth birthday.

And last, my car died a smoky, horrible, screeching death in the center of town last evening while I was car-pooling the field hockey players home from practice. Yes, the university students are back. No, they haven't finished the construction on the main street that goes through downtown. Standing by my car in the middle of that chaos while waiting for the tow truck was an experience. Did I mention it was raining? Did I? The girls called a friend who drives, and abandoned me faster than you can say *Frank's your uncle.*

Oh, and when I get home today I am going to have to take my son aside and tell him it is NOT a good idea to try to show his mother the various places on his body where hair is growing, especially while she's driving. There are some things moms should never see. Ever.

Lesson learned: I'm hoping these are not the best days of my life; otherwise, I'm in big trouble.

Lesson nine

We were working in literacy centers today when I heard Frank's thundering voice from across the room. It's a daily occurrence. He was trying to redirect one of the children in his group to a task that wasn't really PART of the center. A case of the confused leading the even more confused.

I quietly left my own group to walk over and try to right a sinking ship.

"Frank, please remember that Frank worries about Frank, and Suzy worries about Suzy. I, on the other hand, worry about everyone."

"*Crap.*"

"What did you say?" I asked, knowing immediately I shouldn't have asked.

"I thaid crap. Cause I thpilled thome things!"

"Frank. You do NOT say crap in school *or* to the teacher. You never 'crap' the teacher. Do you understand that?" I said convincingly. Or so I thought.

Shrugging his shoulders, he nodded. I walked away and heard him knock over the box containing the one thousand Mr. Potato Head pieces and turned to see them scatter across the floor.

"CRAP!" he shouted, and then looked at me.

I looked and then quickly turned away. Sometimes, just sometimes, you have to ignore the crap.

Lesson learned: Crap is not on our "must spell" list.

Lesson ten

We've spent the better part of two weeks studying apples.

We made apple mobiles. We made apple puppets. We did apple patterning. We sorted apples. We tasted three kinds of apples, graphed our favorites, did a survey, and played an apple game.

We've read *Ten Apples Up on Top; The Apple Pie Book; How Do Apples Grow?; Apples, Apples, Apples; Amelia Bedelia's First Apple Pie; Apples; It's Apple Picking Time; I Am An Apple* and *Up, Up, Up, It's Apple Picking Time*. Just to name a FEW.

Today we finished the unit by making an apple pie in one of our centers. The children rolled the dough, peeled the APPLES, helped slice the APPLES, mixed the APPLES, and filled the pie shell with APPLES.

I walked over to Frank, and looked him in the eye and asked, "Frank! What kind of pie did you make today?"

He swallowed his piece of apple pie, looked at me with a smile and shouted,

"PUNKIN!"

My job is done.

Lesson learned: You say tomato, I say grape.

Lesson eleven

Dear Parents of the Kindergarten Children at Smith and Wesson Elementary,

Yes, we had an AMAZING time on our field trip today to the pumpkin patch. And JUST in case the children are too exhausted to share the details with you, allow me to do the honors.

1. We took an amazingly long ride on the hay wagon to the actual pumpkin patch itself. While no one technically fell off the high and rickety wagon, that does not mean that several boys didn't try their very hardest to accomplish that feat. (Frank.)

2. Each child took his or her time searching the pumpkin patch high and low for a suitable pumpkin to take home. If anyone, and by anyone I mean several anyones, was hit accidentally by flying gourds, I'm sure it came from no one in our own class. (Frank.)

3. We thoroughly enjoyed watching and petting the various farm animals frolicking and playing with each other in the "petting" area of the farm. Yes, the pigs were surprisingly rambunctious, and I'm sure none of the children would have thought that

the pigs WEREN'T playing leapfrog if one of my very street-smart students' hadn't pointed out exactly what was happening. And by the way, Frank, it's not technically called *bumping*.

4. It was an incredible stroke of luck that we were able to see the baby calf that had been born one hour before our arrival. The owner of the farm was so excited about giving us that opportunity and in passing mentioned that *perhaps* the kids might have questions about the mama cow. If any of you have seen what comes OUT of a mama cow AFTER the baby, you have NOT lived. And yes, it was our dear FRANK who pointed it out. I might never sleep OR eat again. You've never seen a teacher move SO FAST to herd the children right back OUT of the barn.

5. The corn maze was incredible. I'm sure Frank is still trying to find his way out. No, Mr. Bus Driver, we only came with eighteen children. You must have been mistaken, now please drive away.

Lesson learned: Always check to see if any cows have given birth before going on a field trip to the pumpkin patch.

Lesson twelve

Top five reasons the teacher is going to the "candy" store tonight:

5. When Frank put his breakfast garbage into its paper bag, the orange juice he neglected to drink spilled out like it was running out of a spigot full blast. He managed to shout the word *crap* and soak the carpet, the class's completed dot-to-dot morning work, Angela, AND Gary. School hadn't even officially begun.

4. When I was putting a few of the completed leaf print journals on the drying rack, I managed to dodge Frank's flying miniature skateboard as it flew across the room in front of me. I had two HUGE green leaf prints across the front of my tee shirt ALL DAY LONG, right on my chest. The most disturbing part of that piece of information - no one on the staff noticed, or seemed to think it was out of the ordinary.

3. The child who is the neediest of all the children in the room, left school today rambling about how all we ever do is *PLAY: play, play, play*! "It's ridikulus!" she said. Did I remind her about our literacy centers, the listening center, the phonics center, Starfall phonics computer game, Calendar Math, math centers, math groups, sorting, and the math game we play every day? EVERY DAY? No.

I gave her a hug and sent her on her way.

2. Carl came to school wearing his Flash Gordon Halloween Costume. While I DID laugh out loud when I saw him, and most of the morning, the fact that "Flash Gordon doesn't HAVE to follow the kindergarten rules" prohibited me from enjoying this new daywear properly. Frankly, I have a Flash Gordon headache.

1. When I went into the kindergarten bathroom in our classroom after school to turn off the lights, I found a cryptic message written in a brown substance all over the outside of the toilet bowl.

It wasn't paint.

Lesson learned: Some days require more medication than others.

Lesson thirteen

I spent most of today trying to redirect my new best friend, Frank.

First, I spent the better part of morning meeting explaining to him why talking about guns, hunting, shooting animals, eating road kill, and how people freeze to death in the winter were not appropriate things to be sharing with your fellow FIVE-YEAR-OLDS.

Then, I had to interrogate him during free play in front of the six (scared) other boys he was playing with until I finally managed to get him to admit that he was talking about bringing in his NERTH gun for tomorrow's show and tell, and not his REAL gun. And yes, he was just kidding when he said there were guns in his backpack. He "meant to thay GUM."

Finally, during math time Alicia informed me that Frank told her and her best friend Kat that he was going to kiss BOTH of them in the coat closet at the end of the day.

"You know Mrs. Marsh, he really, really likes me," she said with a smile and a roll of the eyes.

It took eight minutes of valuable math center time to convince Frank that he was NOT to be kissing the girls, and truth be told they were not his girlfriends at ALL if they

hadn't *agreed* to be his girlfriends.

In the end he just decided to break up with them. Whew.

Lesson learned: Some day I might actually get to teach about MATH.

Lesson fourteen

Every great outlaw had a sidekick, I'm sure; Jesse James, Al Capone, Billy the Kid, Sponge Bob and Bonnie.

Frank's new sidekick is an adorable little fella named Stanley. He's the Abbott to Frank's Costello in every way, shape, and form. While Frank reminds me of a barrel with a Mohawk, Stanley is Alfalfa with glasses, huge blue eyes, and gorgeous blond hair. That's what makes him so dangerous.

All four of the kindergarten classes were outside for afternoon recess. The teachers were discussing last week's somewhat successful field trip while keeping one eye on the playground. Most teachers have developed a unique talent of scanning a playground while carrying on a meaningful conversation. (It's a gift.) My eyes did the quick scan and then I turned my attention back to my own posse.

Ms. Perky, the adorable kindergarten teacher who looks like she's twelve and teaches in the room next to me, glanced at me and said sweetly, "Don't you have Stanley in your class?"

"Yes! He is just **a**-dorable."

"Well don't look **now**, but

that *adorable* boy is peeing in the bushes while carrying on a conversation with the kids on the climbing wall. I'd say that in addition to being cute, he's awfully talented."

"*Stanley*!" I screamed as I went running.

Lesson learned: Remember to put "no peeing outside" to the list of recess rules.

Lesson fifteen

Teachers love to make lists. We make class lists, phone lists, reading group lists, lunch count names' lists, books-we've-read lists, and "what caused the teacher to lose her mind" lists.

Here's *my* list for today:

1. During afternoon centers Frank didn't make it to the bathroom in time and peed all over himself, the floor, and part of the wall. Then, after we ran to get the change of clothes, extra socks, and underpants from the nurse, another child went in and slipped on the "water" on the floor, and HE needed to change.

2. Nick and Ruthie were calling each other bitches at lunchtime. After intense questioning, it was determined that only Nick was calling people bitches. Ruthie only says "shit." Her mom lets her.

3. Frank had a SEVERE meltdown during free play, laid on the floor kicking and screaming, and said he hated school, his teacher (huh?), his whole class, and his cousin Jack. After PLENTY of crying and sobbing, I finally got the bottom of the story. Jay wanted the horned dinosaur instead of the long necked one that Frank was not willing to part with. Frank, in the meantime, had been in three time-

outs since he walked into the room this morning. Things were clearly not going his way.

4. The class bunny, who roams the room freely, managed to get on top of my teacher desk and promptly chewed the special new crayons I had purchased for an activity on Friday and crapped all over someone's behavior chart. Frank had brilliantly kept the teacher preoccupied.

5. The teacher tried unsuccessfully to locate a recipe for RABBIT STEW on the computer because she THREW IN THE TOWEL and took ALL the children outside for recess at 2:00. However, after getting eighteen children zipped, one girl buttoned, locating Taylor's missing glove, and forcing several repeat offenders into the bathroom, we managed only fourteen minutes outside.

I might have lost the battle today, but the war rages on. And as Frank walked out of school today, he turned and shouted,

"This was a great day, wasn't it, Mrs. Marsh?"

Whose room WAS he in today?

Lesson learned: Re-think the whole   class pet idea.

Lesson sixteen

We have eighty-one students in kindergarten this year. They are strategically separated into four classrooms, but invariably one teacher always experiences the class of a lifetime. And that's not always a good thing.

This might be my year.

On our playground is a tall, plastic, "smooth as a sheet of ice" slide that is amazingly popular with most of those eighty-one kindergartners. After climbing the two hundred steps to the top, they fly down the slide at approximately five hundred thousand miles an hour.

What are the odds that one of those eighty-one five-year-olds will kneel at the bottom of the slide to rest his head on the edge and peer to the top and encourage his best friend to slide down?

AND how fast can a teacher with bad knees and a possible hangover run from one side of the playground to the other, watching this scenario unfold in the blink of an eye?

Not fast enough.

And, lastly, out of eighty-one children what are the odds that Frank was directly involved?

But we all know that he is the *one* boy that defies the odds.

Lesson learned: No blood, no foul.

Lesson seventeen

As a class we were discussing the various items that we would be eating for our Thanksgiving Kindergarten Feast. The teachers had already decided what was going to be served, but we like to allow the kids to *think* that they have some sort of say in the matter.

I shared with the children that we would be having some popcorn, carrots and celery, corn muffins, trail mix, and a few other healthy items.

"Boys and girls, can you think of anything else that we should serve?"

Jack suggested turkey, and Judy thought we should have potatoes.

Stanley thought that perhaps we should serve creamed corn, since that's what old people and old pilgrims ate.

Then I saw Frank's hand. "Frank?"

His gravelly voice said, "Thigarettes."

"WHAT?" I asked, SURE I had misunderstood.

"THIGARETTES I thaid." He shouted VERY loudly.

"Cigarettes? You think I should serve Cigarettes?"

"Yeah," he said. "They're candy, and you can puff thmoke out of 'em. They're good!"

Lesson learned: Never, ever call on Frank.

Lesson eighteen

Today during morning "telling sharing" we learned many interesting things.

George played his Wii Star Wars game last night.

James played his Playstation Star Wars game last night.

Douglas played his DS Star Wars game last night.

Frank learned the penetration move in wrestling class last night and jumped up to grab a volunteer so he could demonstrate.

I politely *declined* his offer to show the class. AFTER I had spit out my coffee.

Lesson learned: Always, always check Frank's telling sharing BEFORE he shares. And then refer to lesson sixteen.

Lesson nineteen

Today during Morning Meeting, Michael was pretending to shoot all around the room using a pretend machine gun. He is quite talented in that regard.

I stopped Telling Sharing to point out AGAIN to Michael, and the rest of the class, that we do not talk about violence in school; we don't pretend things that look like they involve violence, etc., etc., etc.

"What's *violence*?" shouted Frank, without raising his hand. He's quite talented in that regard.

I looked at him. "You don't know what violence is?" I asked, dumbfounded. Didn't I just take thirty minutes the other day to convince him that talking about the Chucky movie was not appropriate in kindergarten? "Class, who can tell Frank what violence means?"

Jack raised his hand. "Well, violence is something, it's like, well, The Civil War was *very* violent. It's when people fight and get killed!"

"Yeah!" shouted Gregory, "It's when people hit or kill or kick or shoot!"

When Frank heard that he pointed his finger at me and shouted, "I liiiike it!!"

53

I was not surprised.

Lesson learned: Practice the straight face in front of the mirror one hundred times before coming to school.

Lesson twenty

The following is a delightful note from today's substitute teacher. Some days even the best of teachers get sick. Even if they KNOW it's going to come back to haunt them.

Dear Ms. Marsh,

First, I want to say that I hope you had a great day at your computer training. Thanks for the great plans, and you were right, your paraprofessional is amazing! You have established a great routine with the children and we completed all the morning activities according to your plans. Everything went very smoothly. Well, that is until lunch.

I won't bore you with the details of Frank's antics at lunch, for I'm sure that your paraprofessional and probably the custodian will fill you in about those. After lunch we went outside, and when we were out at recess Frank managed to find the only pieces of ice left on the playground and then proceeded to eat them. They were filthy and disgusting. He refused to give me the remaining pieces and ran circles around me before I convinced him to stop. We managed to get him inside with the rest of the class and got him focused on listening to the story I was HOPING to read to the class.

That was when Stanley and

Frank decided it would be fun to have a wrestling match on the carpet. While most of the class tried to ignore the show, there were several children shouting and watching in delight. I'm sure you know who they are. During this incredible WWIII wrestling match, Suzy decided it would be a great time to dump the entire tub of toys on the carpet in the kitchen area. (How she snuck in there I will never know.) I instructed her to clean it up and returned to the situation at hand (the wrestlers). I got things taken care of, and when I checked on Suzy twenty minutes later NOTHING had been cleaned up. She was, however, having a great time laughing and hiding under the many toys that were covering the floor.

There were several other incidents, but I think you get the picture. An overwhelming majority of the class was beyond excellent today, so I don't want you to think it was just an awful day.

Thanks again, ask me to substitute anytime but just give me a couple of weeks. I love working in your room, even when it's making me feel about eighty years older than I am because it's always interesting, which keeps me on my toes and the kids make it all worth it in the end.

I've decided that this is the year you deserve a GOLD MEDAL. Get hold of me if you have any questions, but not tonight. I am having beverages, and plenty of them.

Lesson learned: Make sure that I don't attend any in-services, trainings, get sick or have my kids get sick at ALL THIS YEAR. Apparently, there are no subs willing to come to my room.

Lesson twenty-one

I thought I knew kind of where he lived.

He rode Bus 45, the one that dropped the children at the housing units on Tulip Drive. I'd known many students over the years who rode that bus, and I always prepared myself for the many surprises and challenges that those particular children might spring upon me, usually when my back was turned. More often than not, they were the ones that made me scream, smile, laugh out loud, and earn every single penny of my paycheck.

Frank made all of them look like rookies.

I left school early that fall day and happened to be behind Bus 45. I made my way slowly down University Boulevard, stopping behind the bus as it deposited children along the way. I realized along the way that Frank was surely riding this bus.

His was the last stop, the one at the corner of University and Tulip. I saw him leap from the bus, land, and roll across the ground. He came to a stop at the feet of a woman I knew had to be his mother. She laughed, reached down for him, and wrapped him in a huge bear hug as the bus pulled away. I pulled into the gas station on the next block and turned to see if I could spot them.

I did.

They hadn't walked up the steps into the housing unit as I had anticipated. Instead, they continued down Tulip Drive and past several small cottages that seemed out of place next to the mammoth apartment complex with which I was so familiar. They turned and walked up the sidewalk towards the pink cottage located at the end of the street. It was a beautiful, well-kept, adorable hot-pink cottage.

Yep. The boy with the crazy Mohawk, press-on skull tattoos, and road kill bones in his backpack lived in a hot pink cottage. It figures.

Lesson learned: Some tales aren't so tall.

Lesson twenty-two

I spent the better part of today convincing the class that contrary to what Frank matter-of-factly announced at morning sharing, Santa Claus was NOT dead.

Oh, and the best way to give the teacher a migraine on the first day back from a five-THOUSAND-day Thanksgiving break? Announce to the class that Santa Claus is dead.

We spent the day trying very hard to remember all of the rules and routines that were erased from their minds by all the turkey, stuffing, potatoes, and time off. We worked very, very hard. My planning something for every minute of the day kept the kids in line (for the most part).

After I had finally managed to erase ALL memory of the "Santa is Dead" incident, Stanley stood up to perform at our closing performance circle at the very end of the day.

He sang a song he composed himself. He called it "Santa Claus is Dead."

Those two have finally decided to play for the same team. It's a @(#*$&@(@* conspiracy.

Lesson learned: Do not let Frank befriend anyone who might possibly be susceptible to brainwashing. Oh, and Stanley is never to sing again.

Lesson twenty-three

My Tuesday To-Do List:

1. Remind Annie that when she changes into her snow pants in the hallway she is NOT to remove her real pants, especially if the principal and two members of the school board are touring the building.

2. Remind Frank and Stanley that the teddy bears are not bad guys and can't be used to shoot the girls dead during free play in the kitchen area.

3. Clearly define the difference between hugging and strangling someone within an inch of their life.

4. Remind John not to leave the bathroom with his pants around his ankles. And tell him to shut the door while he is in there.

5. Have Frank re-do the portrait of his stuffed polar bear. Call me crazy, but a scary vampire bear with blood on his teeth and a Mohawk doesn't even CLOSELY resemble the adorable polar bear that was in his lap.

6. Reinstate naptime, at least for the teacher.

Lesson learned: Keep a HUGE loaf of bread and an extra LARGE jar of Nutella in your desk drawer. You never know when you will need a snack.

Lesson twenty-four

These were the exciting events from TODAY'S morning meeting.

Someone in the group was passing just a bit of gas, and let's just say that it was extraordinary.

Frank, never at a loss for Chris Rock-like one-liners, cried out, "It smells like Nana's pot roast up in here!"

Now, I've never had Frank's Nana's pot roast, but if it even smelled remotely like what we were all smelling, I wouldn't put it in my mouth.

A little voice whispered quietly from the back of the group, without missing a beat...

"Sorry, guys ... my butt's just working overtime." It was our dear little Sam.

Knowing the stomach flu was making the rounds here at school, I kept my eye on little Sam all morning, because noxious gas often precedes a cookie toss...

Sure enough about a half hour later... I beat my fifteen-second "running with the garbage can" record.

And not a DROP made it to the floor.

Lesson learned: Never, ever go to Frank's Nana's house for pot roast.

Lesson twenty-five

Yesterday morning Frank came RUNNING into the classroom.

"I have a present for SUSIE! I have a PRESENT for SUSIE!" He was yelling this to me at the top of his lungs. (And kind of running in place at the same time. Can you picture that?)

"Go out and wait at the coat closets for her then. And remember, she is usually late."

Frank went out to the coat closet, waited for a few minutes, and then ran BACK into the room, yelling the same thing. "I have a present for SUSIE! I have a present for SUSIE!" And then he turned and ran back out to the coat closets.

This went on for at LEAST ten minutes. Which, in kindergarten time is like four hours.

Finally, he came in the room empty handed, stood in front of me and looked at me like he wanted to say something.

"What, Frank? What is it? Did you give Susie her present?"

"Naw. I got TIRED of waiting for her. I just gave it to Hannah." And with that, he turned and sat down.

Tired of waiting, my #**.

Lesson learned: Men really ARE all alike…

Lesson twenty-six

The first day back after a billion-day, action-packed, gift-filled Christmas holiday is a killer. I know, I know, you parents are having a huge "free at last" party, but we were feeling like, well, we were having root canals with no anesthesia.

I gathered the children on the carpet after recess for a Calendar Math lesson and did my best to reel in the munchkins. After finally managing to hook them with a humorous, sing-songy New Year's thingy I asked the all-important question.

"Okay, boys and girls, who can tell me what month it REALLY IS? What is the FIRST month of the year? The one in that song we sing every day? Anyone?"

I looked out at a sea of faces, all the while pointing at the huge word January, and felt like I was speaking Chinese.

"People! Who knows? Anyone? Frank, do YOU know what month this is?"

He looked at me, threw his hands up, and in his gravelly voice said, "I got nuffin."

It's nice to know that singing

that @*#& "Months of the Year" song for seventy-six days has worked so well.

Dr. Jean and your famous CD's geared toward children's learning, you owe me $22.50.

And THEN after talking about what month it WAS, clapping the month, singing the song AGAIN, he looked at me and said, " I nevah HEAWD of it."

I am seriously adopting that kid.

Lesson learned: My lips move, but apparently nothing comes out.

Lesson twenty-seven

At my literacy center today we shared Weekly Readers about Healthy Foods. Thanks to donorchoose.org and the FABULOUS people who made this teacher's dream come true, we receive Weekly Readers every week to support our reading program.

To prepare, I made word cards for some of the words that the children would see over and over. One of them was the word ARE. I showed them ARE; we talked about ARE; we wrote the word ARE and even used magnetic letters to make the word ARE.

Then, we read a poem about healthy food that ended EACH TIME with "Colorful Foods ARE good for you."

At the end of the fifteen minutes of the ARE barrage, I asked the kids how to spell ARE.

Frank immediately raised his hand. "A-S-S."

And so endeth lesson number 4,321,405. (Oh sure, he lisped, but I KNEW what he said.)

Lesson learned: "Ass" is funny, no   matter WHO says it.

Lesson twenty-eight

I went to work this morning full of great expectation, hope, and a thousand prayers.

I reminded myself that each day is a new day, and I had reminded the kids of this as they flew out the door the day before.

The morning went surprising well. Of course, I spent ten minutes before the children arrived frantically scouring the teacher's lounge for help when I was informed again that my paraprofessional sub cancelled. Sure, I had a parent coming to my rescue when I sent an email gently requesting help (TEACHER NEEDS HELP OR ELSE!) but I was counting on that other body to help me live through our rotating reading centers.

It worked, and an angel from heaven came in from another room to pinch hit for an hour. In addition to helping with centers, she also recorded our lunch orders and took them to the cafeteria. (This tidbit will become important very soon.)

I was in a much better mood by Kid Writing, and even Frank's antics during library couldn't dampen my spirits. After all, there are some "things" that are just a part of each day. And most of those things involve Frank.

By the time we went to lunch I was feeling a lot like the woman sliding surprisingly fast down a slippery slope—again.

We went through the lunch line. By some cruel twist of fate Sally, the young lady in our room who is the pickiest eater in the universe, was forced to take a lunch that she did not order. (I didn't go down without a fight—but I lost the battle.)

She was in tears by the time we all got back to the room and sat at the end of a table crying. I followed her back hoping to find some items in our snack closet to ease her pain when Frank walked in behind me.

He placed his tray beside Sally, who was clearly distraught. Her shoulders were hunched, her head was hanging down, and tears were falling on her lunch tray - the tray that contained only the turkey sandwich that she hadn't ordered.

Frank looked at me, looked at her, looked at me, and then back at her. He looked at his tray and picked up his grilled cheese.

"Do you want mine? I'll swap ya."

She looked up and through her tears nodded and began to smile.

Then, I heard a sound. It started softly and ended in an incredible round of applause. Amid the roar, I heard Stanley yell, "FRANK! YOU'RE THE MAN!"

All of his classmates had witnessed his simple act of kindness. And so had I.

He shoots, he shoots, he shoots, and THIS time, he scores.

Lesson learned: You might think you're the teacher, but some lessons are taught by the person you least suspect to shine.

Lesson twenty-nine

I stood in the hallway and watched Frank throw his coat and backpack in the general vicinity of his clearly labeled coat hook. He quickly turned to me, and I could tell he was anxious to share something,

"This morning my cat went to the happy place," he said in his gravelly voice.

"The happy place?" I asked—worried about how this particular cat named "Trouble" might have met his maker.

"Yeah. He gets the blanket and humps it."

"Okay. Well, I'm glad that he's okay," I said as I turned to find a private place where I could laugh out loud.

Lesson learned: What happens in the coat closet clearly stays in the coat closet.

Lesson thirty

The morning after two snow days is always full of animated discussions.

The children were working on their morning seatwork as I took care of attendance and the lunch count for the day.

"I could hardly get up my driveway yesterday after all that ice!" I was telling Mrs. Jones. "It reminded me of when I was stuck in Washington, D.C., last year!"

I heard a voice at my elbow. It was Stanley. "Hey! I used to live in Washington, D.C.!"

"Stanley, I remember your mom telling me you were born here! Were you maybe in your mommy's belly when you lived there?"

"Naw," he said, shaking his head, "I was just a sperm then. A very slow sperm going towards the egg."

And that is how you go from snow to sperm in 9.3 seconds. Let's see Jimmy Johnson do THAT.

Lesson learned: The word sperm is   funny, no matter who says it.

Lesson thirty-one

During morning meeting we had an animated discussion about what the kids wanted to be when they grow up. The discussion then drifted along with us as we started our learning centers.

Daisy asked, "Ms. Marsh, can a woman be president?"

"Yes they can! But a woman hasn't been one yet." I replied.

Daisy then declared, "**I** want to be president some day!"

"That sounds great! It would be fun to run for president…"

"RUN? **RUN?**" she shouted, incredulously. "Never mind then, I can't even jog!"

Lesson learned: Be sure to have more than ONE cup of coffee each morning if you teach kindergarten. You're gonna need it.

Lesson thirty-two

We've had an inordinate amount of celebrations in school during the month of February. We've been planning parties for MLK day, our hundredth day of school (which frankly felt like the thousandth), Valentines Day, and President's Day. We wrap these celebrations with history lessons, craft projects, tons of glitter, math and writing activities. But what do the children remember? The parties.

This morning, the day after Valentine's Day, Suzy came running into school with a worried look on her face.

"Mrs. Marsh, what DAY is it?" she asked, huffing and puffing.

"It's Thursday." I replied.

"But what special day is it?" she clarified. And I reminded her that on Thursday our special class was art.

"No! Are we having a party today?" she continued.

"No. There's no party today." I answered with a smile.

"A snow party?" She asked wide-eyed.

"No…there's no party today." I insisted a bit louder.

"A snow party! A snow party! I love snow parties!" she shouted as she began to dance around the hall.

79

It was then I realized we were having an Abbott and Costello "Who's on first" conversation, and I laughed out loud.

"No, no, no… *No party*. NO! PARTY! TODAY!" I insisted, and she pouted dramatically as she turned to hang up her coat.

To follow the invisible bouncing ball while holding discussions with kindergarteners is a skill that sometimes gets lost amidst all the glitter, cupcakes, construction paper, and glue. These February celebrations have left this teacher a bit "disausted," and so while I shake out the glitter and clean my classroom, I offer these pearls of wisdom for your enjoyment. Just quietly throw a blanket over me and close the door on your way out.

"Mrs. Marsh, I'm trying to make bunny ears on my shoelaces but my thumbs hate that idea. "

"My leg is pretty much broken. But it's okay. I can still run."

"I am not a fancy man. I like to be dirty."

"Frank, are you copying from Emma's paper?"

"Yeah, but only cause she makes it so easy for me."

"Mrs. Marsh, I did not have a very good weekend. I drownded. I'm okay now."

When working on math equations to 15, Sam said, "I know that 105 take away a WHOLE LOT is 15."

"That animal is a manivore. He sneaks at night."

"I think that singing Ghostbusters is better than Christmas Carols."

"Please tell me what to write quick cause in four seconds I forget everything."

"I don't ever get 'stracted by girls."

"I almost popped my eyeballs out last night."

"Frank wrote on the table! Yeah, but it's gone. He licked it off."

"Mrs. Marsh, please tell everyone to be quiet. My arms are sleeping."

"I have been writing 6's my whole life! I am sick of writing 6's."

As we wrapped up our day and the children packed their stuff to go I felt a tug on my sleeve. It was Suzy, the one who was insistent this morning that today was a special day. I spent most of the day redirecting her, reminding her, reprimanding her, correcting her and helping her.

"It was a beautiful day today, Mrs. Marsh! But not as beautiful as you."

Lesson learned: Sometimes the best valentine of all doesn't come in an envelope; it comes from the heart.

Lesson thirty-three

Luke is a bit precocious. He is also just a TINY bit lazy. I often (okay, every ding-dong day) have to persuade him in a firm way to get his work done. Today was no exception.

"Luke, you just have to write a row of 9's and then you're **done**! I know you can do it!"

He wailed in pain, "It's like you're TORTURING ME!!!"

He turned to Suzy and said angrily, "I was having a **marvelous** childhood until all of **this** happened."

That's me. Torturer extraordinaire.

Lesson learned: Learn additional torture methods, and see if the CIA has any openings.

Lesson thirty-four

I spent a few minutes after school today slumped in my rocking chair beside the whiteboard. I was exhausted, as are most teachers the end of the FULL MOON day. You cannot tell me that children don't morph on days when there is a full moon. Teachers KNOW.

I started thinking about what "real" people do during the day, and the things that THEY say while on the job.

Things like, "Nurse, scalpel!"

And, "Trade the stock! Trade now!"

Or even, "Your honor, I object!"

You know what I said today? You want to know ALL THE THINGS I said at work today? Here's what my fried brain remembers:

"Jack, please get the play dough off your head, please."

"Frank, we do NOT talk about C-4 or any other kind of explosives in reading groups: or any other time during our day in kindergarten. Got it?"

"No, Jack, do not make Batman masks out of the play dough."

"Helen! HELEN!!! Do NOT

eat the chicken legs in the play kitchen. They are FILTHY!"

"Rachel, were you sniffing the markers again? Yes, you were! Then why is your nose purple, red, brown, and green?"

"Jack, no more play dough for you! For at least a week!" Mrs. Jackson, did he put that in his pants? Really?

"Frank, do NOT crawl under the table and eat those brownie crumbs! Stop it! There is no ten second rule when the floor is FILTHY."

"People, I am begging you, please, please, PLEASE do NOT put your fingers in your noses. We have five billion boxes of tissues in this room that NO ONE USES. Well, except me."

Lesson learned: Running a marathon isn't the only thing that can wipe someone out.

Lesson thirty-five

We were working somewhat quietly during our literacy centers this morning when we were rudely interrupted.

"Frank!" I asked in a shocked voice. "Was that a burp?"

"Nope. It was a fart that came outta my mouf."

Lesson learned: Yes, sometimes there are stupid questions.

Lesson thirty-six

Frank was sitting at my table coloring this morning. It was 8:40, and I had already assigned him the special seat when I asked a question.

"It sounds like you have a cold! Are you sick?"

"Naw," he said, coloring furiously, "I'm not sick. Boogers just clog up my holes and make me talk funny."

Lesson learned: Sometimes the teacher doesn't learn her lesson. (See Lesson thirty-three.)

Lesson thirty-seven

During snack time I noticed Frank talking intently to Jia, our new little darling from China who speaks NO ENGLISH. He was very intent sounding out what sounded like the nonsense words we had been practicing in centers all year long. Isn't it amazing how he can say them to someone who doesn't understand them?

I watched as he tried to encourage Jia to repeat words that meant absolutely nothing in any language. Jia simply looked at Frank and smiled. I'm convinced that Jia speaks English more fluently than me, and that one of these days she'll recite the Gettysburg Address in front of the class.

"Frank, exactly WHAT are you saying to Jia?"

"I'm teachin' her how to speak fanyish." He said matter of factly.

"How about we stick to English? We'll worry about Fanyish another day."

He then proceeded to count in Fanyish: *uno, doos, trees.*

Lesson learned: Don't allow Frank anywhere near a child who is trying to learn English.

Lesson thirty-eight

Today before I left for the day, I wrote a note to the most incredible custodian in the world.

Dear Jack:

I'd like to apologize for any and everything that you find awry in the room tonight. We had an afternoon filled with planting seeds, constructing buildings for our city, and gluing tissue paper flower projects together.

At the end of the crazed hands-on learning activities that I had stupidly planned for a Monday afternoon, one of my little guys decided that there was no time like the present to get a haircut—from himself.

As I helped Stanley look for his hair under the tables, this provided an amazing distraction for our Frank, who you know all too well. Remember when the bathroom was covered with brown, um, stuff, and you supervised as he cleaned the toilet, floor, and walls? Well, he slipped into the bathroom and got to work again today. Only this time he managed to slather layers of SOAP all over the toilet seat, toilet bowl, sink, and paper towel dispenser.

By the way, I had no idea the

soap dispenser could HOLD that much soap. And neither did he.

I guess you could thank him for making your job just a tad easier tonight. His efforts, however, made my job a tad harder. It's tough to teach a roomful of five-year-olds when tiny bubbles are floating through the classroom. (Cue Don Ho.)

Lesson learned: Cleaning isn't always a good thing.

Lesson thirty-nine

It was a particularly difficult day for Frank. And that means for everyone else.

Sure, we've had more good days than bad lately, and the good ones are okay. But when I say a day is particularly difficult, I mean that he went above and beyond the call of duty in his effort to exact a sabbatical from this seasoned teacher.

After using various not-so-brilliant techniques to get out of any and all work all day long, I finally managed to glue that boy's seat to a chair. Well, with the help of the counselor, principal, and someone by the name of Mom.

He was finally conveniently sitting at my table at the end of the day, completing a project that the rest of the group was working on in the comfort of their very own workspace. Frank sighed dramatically as he cut out the lily pad and looked up at me.

"I was thinking maybe I should try out some of the other teachers."

"Don't think I haven't tried." I muttered under my breath, a bit too quickly.

Then I added with a smile,

"But you know I wouldn't give you up for all the stickers in China."

And at that moment, I almost meant it.

Lesson learned: Sometimes it does take a village, especially when the village has the mom.

Lesson forty

Hmm…let's do a quick recap of the day, shall we?

1. Number of students who had Easter candy for breakfast? An enthusiastic ELEVEN!! A brief note to parents; please, hide the candy the night before the first school day *after* vacation. For the love of ALL that is holy, hide the Easter candy.

2. Number of classroom helpers who couldn't make it to school today? All. While I knew this in advance, it did NOT make the herding of the sugar-coated cats any easier.

3. Number of names that appeared in the "I need to think about what I've done while walking the track at recess"? Seven And let's just say that Easter candy can make even the most incredibly well-behaved children dive headfirst into the dark side.

4. Number of students who took the ketchup bottle at lunch and put said ketchup up and down his arms and down the middle of his head to make it look like BLOOD 'cause it was so COOL? One.

5. Number of teachers with a TAD bit of a headache and a new master plan in order to ensure her possible survival tomorrow?

One.

Lesson learned: Next year, get a sub for the day after Easter vacation.

Lesson forty-one

I start to panic every year at this time. Report cards and parent conferences are right around the corner, closely followed by the end of the year. Every single year I think, "But wait, I still have at least six months of teaching to do!"

I was administering one of about a thousand end-of-the year assessments to my darling Suzy yesterday.

We finished the four-part letter assessment, and I encouraged her to move about the room before we started the number "test."

She suddenly came back to life and chose to twirl and dance about the room. When I managed to coax her to return to her chair, I explained what we were doing next.

"We're going to see how much you've learned about numbers this year! Won't that be fun?"

Suzy smiled and started jumping up and down. "Oh, I am SO GOOD at numbers! Actually, I know ALL numbers! I know ALL THE NUMBERS IN THE ALPHABET!"

Lesson learned: Sometimes it doesn't matter how many days you've been in school, dancing and twirling will still be the most important thing to a five-year-old.

Lesson forty-two

It's the end of May, and we've been in school about one billion and forty-one days, give or take. I finally realized that keeping Frank in his own "learning group" is the very best way to keep him somewhat focused. It might also be the best way to keep the teacher from drinking every night after she gets home from school, although that hasn't technically been confirmed.

However, even when we do whole group lessons or things that don't involve groups, Frank still ends up spending an inordinate amount of time working at my table. Actually, the kids now call it "Frank's table." While most children might not view this as a good thing, he seems to think it's a place of honor. In fact, he likes to call it his "office."

It was near the end of the long and painful day, and we were wrapping up our journal writing. And when I say we I mean he. Him. Frank. He was trying to finish his picture when he held up one of his markers and said in a very professor-like raspy voice, "You know, you can kill yourself by putting a marker in your eye."

I looked at him.

"Frankly," I said, "At this

point I think I'd like to test that theory. On myself."

At 2:30 at the end of a long, long day? Don't think I wasn't serious.

Lesson learned: Exhaustion CAN cause people to consider drastic measures. Pass the markers.

Lesson forty-three

I've been thinking long and hard about how I was going to send Frank off to first grade. A rocket? A bazooka? I realized that sending him on was going to be far more difficult than I had thought because he had found his way into my heart.

I remembered another young man also named Frank who came into my life ten years earlier.

I was teaching second grade. He came to me with a reputation of being "difficult, headstrong and uncooperative." I trusted the comments from his first grade teacher, as she was not only an experienced, amazing teacher, but also a good friend. I knew in my heart, however, that what is a problem for one person can often be a blessing for another.

The first time I sat down with my new second grader, I asked him a question about his weekend, or something mundane like that. He proceeded to tell me about the rise and fall of the Mayan civilization and the ancient Incas. To be honest, I was so fascinated that I sat with him for at least twenty minutes until I realized it was WAY past time to get the children to music and ran them down the hall.

I learned so many amazing

99

things from him that year, and dubbed him our "little professor." I would often defer to him, saying, "Well, class, let's see what Professor Jones thinks about this. Frank, what are YOUR thoughts?" And with a shy smile, he would offer his five thousand cents.

In fact, on many occasions he would say something so brilliant I would point to the door and shout, "PACK YOUR BAGS AND GET OUT! You belong in FIFTH GRADE!" and then the whole class would erupt in laughter as Frank would pretend to leave.

He would also, at times, offer me a challenge and refuse to participate in certain writing activities. I would somehow manage to help him turn it around, I can't remember how, and as the year progressed these events would happen less and less frequently.

It was with amazing pride, and of COURSE a few tears, that I watched him at Daughter 1's graduation weekend. He received the honor of being named the class valedictorian. This, out of over seven hundred very capable students, was quite an accomplishment.

Then last night I received this email.

"Mrs. Marsh, I don't think Frank would mind if I shared something with you. In his college application essay, he wrote about a very special person who made a difference in his life. It was a teacher who turned things around for him, who called him her 'little professor' and was one that he has never, ever forgotten. You do know ... it was about you."

And now as I prepare to send off my new, challenging Frank, I remind myself about life's surprises. I remember that we all have our gifts and our curses.

I just pray that along the way that Frank remembers this kindergarten teacher: the one who loved him first.

Lesson learned: Sometimes the children that punish and challenge you the most are the ones who bring you the greatest reward.

The final lesson

My daughters and I wanted to try the nail salon that was hidden in an obscure shopping plaza a stone's throw from where I live. We were celebrating summer vacation by treating ourselves to a pedicure.

I was thrilled to get a chance to spend time with my girls, now in college, and we agreed to meet there.

The salon is located on the farthest side of town, miles away from my elementary school, and other establishments I was so used to frequenting. I discovered it quite by accident, and I drive by once in a while always considering treating myself. I always talk myself out of it. The parking lot is often empty.

I pulled in alongside one other car and walked into the tiny shop to wait for the girls. I signed in and noticed a woman having her nails done and at least four children of various sizes, shapes, and colors sprawled across the couches and chairs that lined the front of the shop.

My eyes were then drawn to the child huddled at the feet of the woman having her nails done, engrossed with his PDA. He was wearing camouflage pants and appeared to be   sporting a Mohawk.

I shouted his name in a surprised voice, and he turned.

It was Frank.

And in that laughter-filled, loving embrace, I was reminded that even though I never know what might be around the corner, odds are great that it will be something wonderful.

The front cover was designed by Jeff Beck, an artist and musician from State College, Pa, who teaches art to elementary and high school students. He also enjoys playing with several bands in the State College area.